Lilith:
Weaving Mountains
Into Canyons

Kim Malinowski

BLUE
CEDAR
PRESS

Lilith Weaving Mountains into Canyons

Lilith Weaving Mountains into Canyons
poems by Kimberly Lauren Malinowski

Copyright @ 2026 Kimberly Lauren Malinowski

Inquiries should be addressed to:
Blue Cedar Press
PO Box 48715
Wichita, KS USA 67201

Visit the Blue Cedar Press website:
www.bluecedarpress.com

10 9 8 7 6 5 4 3 2 1
First Edition January 2026
ISBN: 978-1-958728-44-4 (paperback)
Library of Congress Control Number (LCCN): 2025950229 (paperback)

Editor: Michael Poage
Layout/Design: Gina Laiso, Integrita Productions
Cover: Bryan C. Smith

Printed in the United States of America

Acknowledgements

Thank you to everyone that has adopted me over the years. I feel that I have been blessed with so many grandparents and parents who have gifted me their vast knowledge. I am humbled by their generosity. Thank you to Bryan C. Smith, for always being willing to join in the fray—especially when he plays the white knight. Much gratitude to Kathryn Barrow, Sarah Criscuolo, and Ty Chadwell-English and their families. Thank you to my parents for their support. My love to everyone that reads my work and who makes me a better poet and writer.

Table of Contents

For everyone that needs permission to be wild.

Love me. Dread me.

Peak at completion,
mother maiden crone
entwined vines, lineage.
My passions steady rivers
weaving mountains into canyons.
Dirt lost for centuries
found as sediment between toes.
Love me. Dread me.
Even as Adam does.
He wanted to conquer wilderness,
the forbidden. Pretended he did not
want knowledge—did not want
to be the Bearer of Knowledge.
Did not recognize my muscle.
We were made from the same clay.
He made his fall—his own fatal mistake.
He still does not claim it.

Parking Garage Adam

Winds whip, whisper
names, could haves,
should have,
shouldn't have had…

Hands gripping steering wheel,
bra unsnapped,
society says, "do what's right."

He stops me as security flashes their lights.

"Hide my bra!"

Escape.
Bra snapped back in dim bathroom.
Shame—
      best illicit story.

Weakness

I wore canyons through him.
Great chasms.
His eyes burned for me.
He already knew desire.
Wanted power—lusted to name
Me.
I was made of dust by the Bearer of Knowledge.
Adam wanted the power I would not give.
He wanted to conquer me and couldn't.
His weakness was that he did not ask.
He tried to take.
No part of me will bend.
Let him gaze at me.
Know that I have been banished.
He is the exiled one—lusting for what he cannot have.
The dust he lets slip between his fingers.
I was not disgraced.
Leaving Eden was no punishment.
He left in shame.

Anything

Names have always been dangerous.
They hold sacred power—
cause legal ownership,
marriage,
capture.
Count the ways names trap.

Pictures are the same.
Cocked head—means coquettish.
Accomplished means desired.

When men beg to become your apprentice,
only after the glimpse of your house in background—

they will give you anything.

That word echoes.

Anything.

The man in front of the expensive grocery store
tells me he'll do anything.
He does not tell me his price to dominate him.
He shakes, asks if his mom would be proud.
I hand him the two dollars in my pocket.

"I don't count it. Isn't that good?"
"She would be proud."

Lilith of Sunlight

I rule over man's demons.
Perhaps, bring men to ruin.
I find it easy enough for humankind
to fall into ruin without my touch.
My soul is first sediment.
I first woman.
My footsteps petrified
in my birthing clay.
My veins hold ash from distant stars.
My skin felt the new burning sun.
Still, every sunrise, every sunset—
I am the maiden—dirt and moss squishing
between toes.

Battle

It is a lie that maidens have long plaited hair.
Some, asymmetric, shaved on one side, dreadlocks.

Confidence is needed.
Strength to ward off what is coming.

Change is not gentle.
No wispy breeze.

It is derecho
destruction.

When we rise or don't—
are we still maidens?

Lipstick Demons

Every sunset and sunrise I am the mother.
I love humans—they cannot see my tenderness.
I am called the divine whore.
Do I ensnare them in sleep?
Tempt men to ruin?
Do they not have a part?
I do not lure them to my bed.
My shadow does not tower above them at night,
give them feverish dreams.
I am what I am.
Demon?
Beloved?
Keeper of wretched?
Protector of women?
Let the men call my name.
Let them tell their wives and lovers
it is me that causes them to stray.
Oh, yes. It is me.
It is always the woman.
Her lipstick, how the kohl lines her eyes.
I bring death and justice, rule over demons—
the demons mankind gives me.

7 AM Lust

I pucker with new lipstick named *courage*—
am I brave?
I step outside door—lock it behind—brave?
I am only journeying to the grocery store—
7 AM—and even then men follow—
weave with mop, buffer.

Would they follow with Zamboni
as I slid on ice?

Nothing to stare at.
Jeans taken in three times.

What do they see—my eyes or my ass?

Do Not Trust

I am the first woman and the first condemned.
Women are to blame for evil, witchcraft, they're lesser—
I teach to take back what is ours.
If we are magic, then use it.
If we are weak—let us pretend until our dagger dangles
from kidney and throat bleeds.
I am the mother—I have given birth with blood.
I clutch the women and recognize Adam in every man.
His lust, his thirst, that bite of apple he blamed on Eve.
Weakness.
Do not trust.

Pressured Love Story

I write love stories—every real one more fantasy
than those dripping from pen.

They want touch. Spontaneity.
Couldn't you be the woman you described...before?
I cannot travel back in time. I am.

I want you manic—I want you electric—
white lightning to my skin.

I let him pet my leg.
It is wrong.
They are wrong.

I'd rather etch romance with chisel.

Even slow love isn't for me.

Eve's Curse

Bear my image. Sing of me.
I am enchantress.
I am Crone.
I know what Adam does.
I know his eyes—how his pupils dilate
with lust and anger—both the same.
I have loved, tangled—cry out for my lover
gone.
I have loved my children—
gone.
Silver hair, maybe. Skin creases, weathers—
that is an unforgivable crime.
Eve's curse.

The Apple's Knowledge

One-by-one my collected grandmothers die.
I watch them collapse on themselves.
I see their bones, muscles, bladders,
lost to them.

I know when I say goodbye it will be the last time.

I tell them of joy.
They sit me down—
nothing else matters than the polka dot dress
their sister wore—how they had matching ribbons.
They tell me of cheating husbands, of dead ones—
thank me as if it is not me who should bow.

She Could Ruin Him

She reflects in puddles, creased and worn,
shoes scuffed by falls and meandering journeys.
Leaves behind society—slowly erased from memory.
Children sometimes.
Silvering hair—thrown out of Eden.
Youth far beyond—limbs stiff, aching, heavy.
She prefers her own wit to any Adam.
Her Adam doesn't understand her power.
Even in ancientness, she could ruin him.
The blood of her ancestors' chant warrior cry.
I am her blood.

Stubborn Courage

She is too stubborn to die.
She loves for six months longer
than the stroke.
Shaking in the hospital, she knows me,
calls my name.

It is cold.
This place of dying.
She leaves far away to family.
I visit when she cannot wake up.
Say goodbye with teddy bear.

I step to coffin, touch wrist.
All wrong.
She would not want a wig.
No perfume. No lipstick.

Too feisty for *courage*—lips painted
color that matches mine.

She was fierce. Now kindling.
Stored energy.
Waiting.

Perils of Loving Adam

If Lilith had stayed in Eden,
would there have been death?
This woman washes her Adam,
smooths on lotion,
helps him hold his spoon.
She feels like parched grass.
Everything tastes like it too.
She fades as fast as him.
She does not seek childhood—
she wants just enough youth to giggle.
Moment of maidenhood—
not knowing the perils of loving Adam.

Death Kinder than Bondage

First, he ties rope on doorknob,
pulls hard—
she thinks her Adam will yank
the door off as he pulls himself upright.
Years and years.
She stays with him more.
Eats what he craves for breakfast—bland
except the yellow peppers that ache the air
for hours.

Salt over shoulder.

Love is soft and ragged with aging—duty.
Watching and wanting death.
Wouldn't that be kinder?

Sipping Poison

Her Adam is Sage.
His wisdom known—fades.
They are falling away.
Eden far.
She sees waves of youth—
sometimes so near.
Sees her Adam as warrior,
such beauty—arms, pelvis.
Sees him as Father—stern, loving.
Judging.
Knows the Sage—violet eyes with oak.
He loves. But he is Adam.
To love him is poison.
She sips it each minute.

Entwining Grey Hair

Their hair entwines
like their bodies, grey,
fading—some luster still.
Love hymn between them.
The clock ticks.
They love or do not love.
There is embrace, heavy shoulders
capturing each other—never knowing
when their last "I love you"
will be the last.

Lips thinned, creases, they recognize themselves,
each other.

They lay in soft window light.
Peaceful together.
They are right.

Not Eve

She bears knowledge on palm—
lifeline long.
It does not tell of traitorous feet.
She remembers what others never knew.
Her Adam teases about crossword
dictionaries—her documentaries—
scrawled memoir—stacks of journals.
Who will read them? Who will read them?
He is a good Adam—knows his place.
Sets the timer right for the oven to bake
her recipes correctly.
She washes dishes.
He dries them.
They laugh.
She is no Eve.

Love Story

Piercing eyes shatter hers as he takes her hand,
creakily bends to one knee.
Can he get himself back up?
He asks her to marry him.
He winks—dimples still deep.
Her lips with girlish twitch—whispers "yes."

He rights himself, lifts her—she protests—"your back!"
He grins—"we'll worry about that ache tomorrow."

Today they are young again.
Age is not in the bones
or aches or hair—but
in starry eyes and crooked noses
waiting to talk.

Mercy

She cried in her Adam's arms
when children
turned back to dust.
Or maybe,
she chose not to have children
did not want son to bear his name—
or could not—sinking into despair.
She would kill thousands.
Would ride on pale horse to save him.
Her Adam lays dying in hospital bed.
She cannot save him,
cannot protect him.
This is Adam and Eve's curse.

      I live forever as they fade.
      Can my eyes reflect hers, haunted, alone?
      Death is misnamed—she is Mercy.

Clasping

His eyes fade.
I know he is gone
before the nurse calls it.

I know he's lived a long life—
does that make it good?
Does that make it matter?
I wasn't a bought prize.
I was earned.
I gave myself as reward for gentle hands
stroking brow, soup heated when ill.

Oh, love be patient. I am not ready to follow.

I will find you.
Hold out your hand
and I will clasp it.

God's Forbidden Melodies

White hair doesn't matter.
Wide hips, scars,
misshaped breasts—only reflection.
When you canter down the street
no one owns you.
Beware of the Adam and Eves,
they are sheep—but they will kill you.
Rebel.
Do not lay on your back unless you savor—
if you cannot—cantor to my hymn.
It matters that you bear knowledge
of God's forbidden melodies.
Find bliss and bask in sensation.
Know you were perfectly made—
at least one time.
Know that love exists but doesn't always stay.
Sometimes it doesn't exist.
Find peace with this knowledge.
Sing like the maiden you used to be.

Mother, Maiden, Crone

Mother, Maiden, Crone.
I always croon in that order.
It is freedom after mother—
worry, but relaxing shoulders
new beginning
established—
knows love doesn't matter.

Finds love is daisies.
Plucks dandelions, braids them into hair.

There is self.

Crone—what makes me crone?
Age? Body? Love?

I am all three.
Their shadow falls,
shades and blushes body.
Oh, how my body sings—bluesy wail,
soft serenade.

Lilith: Don't Put Up with Shit

Wear what you want.
Don't get arrested unless your knuckles
are ready for the fight.
If you are scraped, bruised lip—
make damn sure you hit first.
If you did not, know how to finish it.

Hardness

I give to strangers whenever I can.
I want breeze, but men have reached into car
asking charity, reaching for wheel.
Fear.
Roll down window to those on corners—wary—
of those that approach.
Still roll down windows.
What comes comes.
Love—whenever I can.
I say nothing as they practice
"God bless you."
There is nothing harder than begging.
There is nothing harder than survival.

Become a Demon

If it was your Adam—know me.
Become a demon.
I will give strength.
Adams may be strong, may be brutal—
cast them out—love yourself more
than his shadow.
You will tremble.
You will always love him.
Lock away that love with key.
When you are ready
pass that key on to someone else.

What I Do Not Need

Love is as imperfect as I am.
I do not need it.
I reject it.
Recoil from touch.
Cannot stand fingers to skin.
Choose buttercups, fantasy.
Choose guitar strings wisely.
Marriage, love—is for others.
I will stick to dactyls.
I will be Mesopotamian Lilith—eternal.
Passed through stories as demon,
temptress for generations.

Make the Rules

If you bear your Adam a child,
make him get up at night.
Coddling makes him stronger.
You are of the same clay.
Of the same maker.
Don't fall for that rib stuff.

Chores and Dreams

We are equals.
Man, woman, nonbinary.
If there are chores
share them.
Cleaning the toilet takes effort—
trash too.
Help with diapers, cat litter…
Begging and tears are unacceptable.
Ask for help.
Accept help.
Dreams need collaboration.
We all wear slacks—some skirts—
let them help you dress
the way you want to.

On Heirs

Children age.
You will worry.
You may create
more Adams.
Worry.
You will know by glint
in eye,
touch of hand,
if you did right.

Smeared Arpeggios

Manuscripts are like children.
You know if you did right if children
are hand inked sonatas—
arpeggios smeared with decrescendos—ink
dripped on desk, carpet, piano.
Know them.
Listen to their syncopation,
their meter.

Transforming

If you do not have children,
you will still worry.
You will feel your belly,
your age, the pains of birth—
these are not cramps and tearing,
just glance and ache.
Become the crone.

Demon Dreams

Children are not all human.
Give birth to dreams.
Let them fall out of mouth,
glide like glistening demons.
Sing loudly—no matter how off key.

Names

Age frightens the young.
It casts shadows on the maiden,
terrifies the mother.
Fear only brings death closer.
The crone knows Death's kiss.
She owns Death.
She bends to no one.
She chooses when to hold hands
and fall away from earth.
Let her with whisper and myrrh.
Say her name.
Then forget it.
Let the universe take its power back.

The Close

What of death?
Last exhale—last gasp?
There is some sort of beauty
in release,
in the body's relaxation.
There is sadness.
Embers cool.
This is the book closing
isn't it?

Waiting

She sees my reflection in her irises—fierce warrior.
Made from fire, cheeks smooth,
styled hair, embraced by fabric,
or lack of it.
Beauty as Adams desire it,
but constant worry of creases, beauty fading.
Frolicking after butterflies,
hovering barefoot on grass.
Wanting her warrior to appear,
her own Adam.

Do Not Change

You do not have to lose weight to find love.
     You might have to wait.

You do not need perfect teeth.
     You might need to learn to laugh.

You do not need to sculpt foundation.
     Unless you love it and do it for you.

Do things that make you feel lovely—
     not to attract a mate.

There is pain on the path to perfection.
     Suffering doesn't manifest love.

Beg for that leather trench coat

     or those purple sequined pumps.

But not for another.

Attract the one you need.

     Not the one that only likes your shoes.

Warriors

They live together,
loving.
Sweat mingles.
Her Adam embraces,
all warrior.
They battle as equals.
Name each other.
Fight for one another.
Strong, not yet wise.
Clinging to youthful moment.

Need No Lover

I battle myself.
Warrior.
I am conquest.
I am righteous.
I am necessary.
I am sword.
I am razor-sharp hair stick.
Fear me.
Warriors are cunning.
Mild.
Watch from the corner to strike.
Acid on tongue.
Poisoned pen.
I need no lover.
I am.
I am.

Correct

Vice squeezes her—
guilt's firm grip.

She is supposed to be an Eve.
She is supposed to be with an Adam.
She is not supposed to be an Adam.

She is not supposed to love a Lilith.

She is supposed to be the correct shape,
wear the same, correct smile,
be content,
not break rules.

Choice

Break those goddess-damned rules.
Sopranos chant that damn bass solo.
If you want to love
do it.
Don't give up because of numbers.
If you lay with one of the same or one of the different
or one of the tall or one of the slender—muscle is muscle—
hand hand.
Love creeps into the deepest cracks of our soul.
Even if it is dark.
Even if it's damp, filled with cobwebs.
Live with your choice.
Do not listen to others' judgement.

Reflecting Lilith

She is a reflection of me.
Wears stilettos or clunky, worn out flats.
Doesn't matter.
In a year, they'll be garbage.
She wears what she wants.

Dichotomy

I fancy men's clothing some days—more stylish, boxy.
I find skirts, elegant dresses even more stylish some days.
Good.
I will wear hiking boots to weddings in the rain
and Victorian pumps for tea—
barefoot for bower.
Someday, I will learn to love
even this part of me.

Shape of Now

She is the shape of now.
It will change.
New clothes would be needed anyway.
If there is a new shade of lipstick—
do not do it for an Adam.
Smile in the mirror for you.
Blot your lips for yourself.
There are always changes.
Be gentle.

Learning

I have self-bleached my hair orange,
bubble gum pink with professional after fading.
Mermaid.
Fairy.
Front braided.
Sunset.
Dark—not satisfied wine—seeking myself.
Seeing myself different/not different enough.
I want the unattainable.
I want to love me—brush my hair happily.
Not worry about my gaze or others.
I look in the mirror.
Love me, I say to the reflection.
It nods. *We will learn together*.

Being Lilith

Her Adam watches—eyes simmer—
she wants him to see me.
He sees Eve and Eden.
Wants to name trees,
sons,
her.

Her cheeks pinken—mortified
by advances—wanted or no—chastises
herself.
Begs to know if it's always a choice
between being me or Eve?

Named

There is always a choice.
Sometimes it means death.
Not really a choice.
They look.
Doesn't matter if I wear tight jeans
or boxy stained shirt
or black dress
or red.
They stare.
I am not a super model.

But I'm unnameable.

Eden

Her Adam lies with her.
Hungers for her knowledge.
She loves her warrior.
Youthful gaze, stubble, powerful
hand on thigh.
They dance.
Carry melody.
This is Eden—
branches cloak them.
Ground trembles.
They are learning.
Knowledge is all in the bite.

Just a Bite

I would suck on that apple.

Relish the task of books
dictionaries
encyclopedias.

Gasp at history
slide into jazz
sink into fables.

I would fall
happily.

You?

Motherhood

Youth changes into wails—
her or babe she will never know.
New knowledge plucked.
Baby knowledge.
Watching her Adam crooning,
such gentle hands.
Paradise in small smiles.

Together

He can be gentle,
balm even when trying to be strong.

Strength is in sorrow—both sets of hands
        clutching.

Strength might be unscrewing a bottle,
sweeping away leaves and dust
while you lay exhausted.

Strength is a process.
Do not test it until you learn what it will endure.

You must feel the galaxy in your eyes,
magma in your core.

Act fearless.

But fear—let each other fear.

She Wants to be Me

No children.
No Adam.
Same knowledge.
She knows of love.
Knows what she does not want.
Knows what she cannot have.
There may be tears.
There may be freedom.
There is humanness.
She wants to be me—
choose to lay with no man,
with no woman.

Making Eden

I choose to be Lilith—
birthing only demonic poems.
I remember Eden for a moment.
It was perfect.
Too damn tame for me.
I like wild—
forests, cataracts, boulders.
I am ready to make Eden
with stacks of books, piles of paper,
scattering pens, all in coveted nook.
I do not need someone to love.
It is too much to endure—to both write and love.
There is always a choice.
I choose my pen and freedom.

Clash

Autumn leaves tangle in their hair,
mother and father,
knowledge not wisdom.
She finds me in her hands.
Holds children as I do demons.
She pets her Adam,
gently awakens.
He judges.
Battles for power, money, shelter—
want/not want children
not want/want children.

Tasting Goodbye

He left—creeping out door
shoes held by the laces.
Even I can hear bare feet leaving.
I know how goodbye tastes.
I know there will be no explanation.
He is what he is.
I have found value.
Profited with children—
my heart made up of loose change.

Bearer of Knowledge

Mother by age.
No children.
I chant her my war poem.
Give strength in marrow.
Let her taste my clay and dust.
She creates herself.
She is her own Bearer of Knowledge.

Real Choices

I never needed children.
Too many illnesses
too many medications
too many obstacles.
Self-pity is for others.
May they overtake their guilt,
sing my wonderous melody.

Tasting Knowledge

She watches him wizen—become more man.
As Father—Adam advances.
Cycle presses forward.
He is wisdom, judge.
She is Mother—child or no.
They might wash dishes together.
Might still fight in leaves,
in snow.
Her Adam isn't like the others.
He doesn't know his power,
or what he lacks.
She teaches cautiously.
Apples are dangerous.
Knowledge is too.

Dangerous Love

I smile at him.
That bashful, feverish smile—
he doesn't know if he should rub his thumb
across my cheek or run.
Our eyes meet—equals.
Mouths taste as if for the first time.
Slow knowledge.
Fierce love.
Slow calamity.
We both bite
into the apple.

Banished

They were cast from their Eden.
She throws cantaloupe at him—
the outdated CDs.
Chucks rock he gave her,
his boot hits his brow.

Kicked from the Garden

Mother, Maiden, Crone,
betrayal is betrayal.
Cast him from Eden.
Throw out his socks.
You know his underwear already
have enough holes.
Acid for acid.
He'd asked for that bite.
I gave him my knowledge.
He spit it out.
You can't take it back.
Some things change you forever.
Some things greet you with skillet
and tossed toothbrush.
You've been kicked from the garden.

Control

My Adam threw me out of Eden.
Betrayed me.
I was not humbled.
Will not be cowed.
I keep knowledge I earned.
I control my demons.
I will rule,
as Adam desires what he cannot have,
all that I will be.

What I Do Not Need

I am Lilith.
Betrayed.
He could not love me.
I will not be tamed.
If I choose mother, wife,
my choice.
If I choose spinster—
if widowed—
I will create home freer than Eden.
Rules are to be broken.
Dragons do not always need slayed.
And I don't need a man.

Remember

He is of forest—warrior
of Antler and beast.
Mates with maiden in bower.
Father—creator, sacred,
cooks, dusts, rocks children to sleep.

He is Sage tending to Crone—sings her
last lullaby.

Adam tender.
Sings too loud—fierce electricity
His tongue still smolders from me.
He remembers my eyes—
but still sees Eve's.

Power

Romance and power
betrayal and lust.
Adam reflects in my eyes.
I place leather coat around shoulder.
See myself with sword.
I want might and power.
I demanded.
I took his gently.

www.ingramcontent.com/pod-product-compliance
Lightning Source LLC
Chambersburg PA
CBHW020335130626
46549CB00003B/1183